The Stylish Mum

A Mum's Guide to Everyday Style

The Stylish Mum:

A Mum's Guide to Everyday Style

TOYA STYLES

ISBN-13: 978-1-387-22355-8

Edited by: Maurisa Coleman Inc.
Cover Photography by: Aaron Musgrove

Book Available at:

TheStylishMom.co
PrettyButter.store
Amazon.com
Lulu.com

Blog:

PrettyButter.com

DEDICATION

This book is dedicated to my Husband for never letting me sulk for too long, and always asking me where's my lipstick and earrings.

And to my little miracle Nadia for her bright smile and unconditional love.

ACKNOWLEDGMENTS

To My Grandmother who has always been a staple in my life pushing me to be greater, I Love you!

To all the fabulous mums out there that are fierce and not afraid to show off!

CONTENTS

1: THE STYLISH MUM METHOD

One of the most defining moments of a woman's life is motherhood. Suddenly, life is not just about you. Everything takes a backseat to your kids. More responsibilities, dependents, and demands all take a toll on your time. The good thing is, the birth of your children does not mean the death of your stylish years. Trust me on this.

Who am I? I am Toya Styles and I run ChicDivineStyle Consulting. My company is a full service fashion styling and marketing consulting firm. Fashion is my first love, consulting is second and beyond a passion for me. It's my soul's calling. For years, I've styled women who needed a "wardrobe intervention" in time for a special event or a wardrobe audit. What fuels my love of styling others are clients seeing their own beauty for the first time or in a new way. Often we hide our best assets due to comments from others. These remarks are commonly from people who are uncomfortable with their own appearance. So much so that it causes us to also feel uncomfortable when we hear their criticism. The effect is: Instead of embracing our bodies and accepting the truth of our own beauty, we hide.

That's where I come in. My strategy is to set your style free. It's about coherence and congruence. What do I mean by that? Coherence is when the external appearance is a reflection of the internal. Congruence is about how authentic and genuine your style is to who you are. That's why dressing up to resemble someone else can look fabulous but feel uncomfortable. True style is about being comfortable in your own skin.

What sets me apart from other stylists is that I see every client as one-of-a-kind. I could simply fashion a person after a famous celebrity and pull it off. However, Judy Garland once said, "Better to be a first-class you than a second rate someone else." My personal commitment is that every one of my clients walks away a first class version of themselves instead of an imitation of anyone else!

I walk my talk, seriously! I'm a stylist and also a proud Air Force wife with two beautiful children. While raising a family I earned a BA in marketing and business management then an MBA. Credentials were important to me because I wanted to be a role model for my kids.

Beauty and brains are a potent standard. Being a mum never means you can't look and feel like a star!

The Stylish Mum was written to show you how to unleash your inner Fashionista. I wanted to share my knowledge with those mums searching for their own look who don't have a stylist. Being on a budget doesn't prevent you from looking like a million dollars.

Never underestimate the power of feeling beautiful in the clothes you wear. The magic ingredient behind every one of my styling projects is to make sure YOU (the client) knows that you deserve to look and feel your very best. Every day is a special occasion to shine. Why? YOU are the role model your children look to. When the client feels beautiful inside out, it's a success.

Impeccable style is about being smart with your time. Once you know what makes you feel beautiful and looks good on you then your shopping trips are more effective. You won't waste time trying on the wrong clothing. Instead you target the clothes that bring out your best assets effortlessly. The right items in your wardrobe means that looking fabulous happens in under an hour. It's a myth that looking good involves copious amounts of time getting ready. Busy mums armed with the right ensemble can look runway ready in under 30 minutes, I can show you how.

2: YOU ARE THE PRIZE

Remember the Prince song "Little Red Corvette?" If not, listen to the tune, and think about how people treat a luxury car different from a beat-up truck. Now imagine yourself a Mercedes or your favourite car. How would you expect people to treat you? This should be easy to visualize. Why? Because YOU are worth it!

As Mums we kick butt. WE do a lot and most of the time we are doing things for other people, mainly our children and significant others. Mums are selfless and sacrificing. We wear many hats to make a household work. Whether you are a stay-at-home mum or work outside the home, motherhood is the hardest job of all. Most of the time, mums think of themselves last. Their reliability, love, and dedication are just some of the reasons why we are so worth it. Mums set the example for their children, set the atmosphere in their home, and love their husbands/significant others. We do so much for everybody else that it's easy for us forget about ourselves.

So why don't mums feel worth it all the time?"

The majority of the time the mum is the financier of the family. We see where money goes. Mums put their children first because they feel that money is better spent on kids, the household, their husbands, many things other than themselves. Mums usually put their stuff on the back burner. It's easy to put off self-care, getting nails done, going for a spa date because we think, "Oh, I'll wait until next week," or, "I don't need to go." Sometimes it makes sense but that's not always the case. We are worth it. For all the giving that a mother does, she deserves to replenish herself and that's one of the reasons I wrote this book.

I've seen so many mums that are constantly setting everything aside in favour of everyone else and rarely invest in themselves. Regardless of what we think it's not fair to them and their families. Sacrificing yourself until you are running on empty is not how it's supposed to be. Associating motherhood with martyrdom simply bothers me. However, it's the very thing that makes mothers so special. When a mother places her family and children before themselves it's because we are committed to the long haul.

Switch Your Sense of Self-Worth ON!

Time to pivot your perceptions about how precious you really are! Time to brainstorm. Answer the following questions and see how it unfolds.

Step One

Right now, list the top 10 moments in recent memory of the many times you were "Supermodel Mum". For example, when you came through for your children, spouse, family, mates, all in a day's work. Give examples of why you prioritized others needs over your own. Make note of what you sacrificed in order to make it happen. Don't stop until you have listed 10 items.

1.	
2.	
3.	
4.	
5.	
6.	
7.	
8.	
9.	
10.	

Step Two

Take a look at your list of achievements. Now, for every item in your list, reflect objectively. Think to yourself, if this was written by someone else, what kind of conclusions would I make about the kind of person these actions are describing? Again, don't stop until you have an answer for all 10 items.

1.	
2.	
3.	
4.	
5.	
6.	
7.	
8.	
9.	
10.	

Step Three

Review your answers in step two and select 5 words that stand out to you. Don't stop until you have completed the exercise.

1.	
2.	
3.	
4.	
5.	

Step Four

Now, if you were to meet any person with these qualities, and you had a budget of £1 million, write down ways that you

would show your appreciation. These gifts would be anything related to self-care to vacations to hiring a nanny to give you a date night. Get creative! Write down all your ideas until you are done.

1.	
2.	
3.	
4.	
5.	
6.	
7.	
8.	
9.	
10.	

Step Five

Finally, create a collage of the ideas you just came up with. If you use Pinterest, create a board just for this (check out my Me Time board on Pinterest). Then, to finish up, create another vision board. If you are using Pinterest you can set these boards to private.

This second board has pictures of you. Under each image copy and paste a sentence from each of the 10 descriptions. Print it out when you are done and post it near your mirror. Better yet, put it in a lovely frame, and hang it near your bed, loo, mirror, or wardrobe.

Make sure it's located where you can't help but see it every day. For the next 30 days look at it and read at least one sentence daily. By the end of the 30 days, you should have read every one of the 10 sentences at least three times. The key is to look at the list before getting dressed!

YES! Do you see how fabulous you are? I bet you had words like Loving, Reliable, Stable, a Rock (Star), Comforter, Compassionate, Caring, etc. in your lists. This is you! If no one has said it "You are a GREAT mum!"

3: FROM SINGLE TO MUM

Remember Your Pre-Mum Days?

Back in your pre-mum era AKA single days, there were days when you could indulge hours getting ready for a night on the town. Everything was about you. No kids or husband to take up time on your calendar. If you wanted to sing an extra hour in the shower you did it. When you decided to prance around the living room while trying on eight different outfits even though you were running late, it didn't matter. Life was all about you. Pre-babysitters, all the time you had belonged to only you.

When I was single I would go to the mall every Friday to pick a new outfit for the weekend! There were no kids to drop off and pick up or dinner to cook. And Lord knows you could try on a complete outfit with no interruptions. No dependents meant more disposable income. We had extra cash to burn on boots and cocktails. Ah yes, those were the Sex and the City days.

Now let's fast forward to a few years later. You found "the one", got "the ring", walked down the aisle, moved in together, and a few deliveries from the stork later, things have changed.

Ready to begin?

The Stylish Bump: Expecting Style for Mums to Be

Congratulations! A bundle of joy is on the way and you're clueless on what to wear anywhere. I faced this. Most women do. Being pregnant means a rapidly changing body that gets bigger by the day. Your old clothes don't fit and the maternity collection may be lacking variety where you live. Relax and see this as an opportunity to get creative while your body changes. You wonder how big you'll get so you're afraid to buy something new. You worry you won't fit into your old skinny jeans post-baby, so all your old clothes are packed away. Don't worry about the temporary changes to your body. Just explore the stylish possibilities and creative potential with maternity wear.

Budget with a Bump

Maternity clothes are far more stylish now compared to when I was expecting, almost a decade ago. Living overseas in Japan the choices in maternity clothes was very limited. However, with a little artistic ingenuity and experimentation, I still stayed stylish. As you only need them for a couple of months, my advise is to bargain shop.

Before you go shopping do remember that pregnancy is a temporary nine month situation. I don't see the point in spending a lot of money on maternity outfits that will become obsolete once the baby is born. When I was pregnant with my daughter I refused to buy any maternity clothes. True story. In fact, I was so stubborn that I wore my husband's clothes towards the end of those nine months. My entire wardrobe was filled with clothes that were too small but I wouldn't budge. I wasn't going to be pregnant forever but I still wanted to look cute with the baby bump. So I improvised and started wearing my husband's white vests. Sad, I know!

Then a good mate noticed my cuteness factor had decreased and brought over a bag of her old maternity clothes. She made me promise to return them since she planned on having more babies. That was my A-HA moment. I couldn't believe it! The light bulb turned on she had solved the problem and didn't even know it. This would save women so much money if they would consign or swap their maternity clothes.

I am pretty sure this was not an original idea but I was living in Northern Japan at the time. I had an epiphany for money savings tips for mummies to be.

However, if you're planning on having more children, then investing in quality maternity clothes you'll wear again makes sense. Working mothers who want to add contemporary pieces to their maternity wardrobe can select a few strategic items to upgrade their styling options.

Nowadays there are some very trendy online maternity boutiques that save you time and money. Check out websites like PinkBlushMaternity.com, Asos.com and Seraphine.com for ideas. There are amazing finds at local stores like Old Navy, Motherhood, and Target. You have many options today compared to when your mum was expecting you. Modern-day dressing up with a bump has plenty to choose from to show off your pregnancy with style!

Mummies-to-Be Money Saving on Maternity Wear Tips Sheet

1. Hold a clothes swap with women who have already had their babies and those who are expecting. This way the expecting mums get maternity gear and the new mums get some new clothes to wear!

2. Find consignment shops that carry maternity wear where you can trade in old clothes and purchase new ones at a reduced price.

3. Shop clearance for clothing that will transition with you after you have the baby. Like button down shirts that can become belted dresses after you have the baby, a nice oversize jumper that can be worn with leggings post-pregnancy or maxi dresses that can be belted or altered after delivery.

4. Altering present clothes and shoes can aid in getting more wear out of them while pregnant. Clothes can be

let out or in as needed. You can add gel insoles and moleskin to the insides of shoes to make them more comfortable instead of buying new ones.

5. Use accessories to change your look. Add a scarf over a plain white vest to add a pop of color.

6. Finding a bump friendly swimming suit can be daunting. Some alternatives are to flaunt your belly and wear a two-piece, throw on a tank top and work out shorts.

7. Cute shoes are a plenty at low prices. Do not shy away from a brightly coloured flat or leopard print kitten heel.

8. You can still be sexy and pregnant. Try a cute sheer babydoll or just silky tank dress.

Baby Is Here!

Congratulations! Your baby is finally here! Time to spend bonding, resting, and delighting in your little wonder that you created and birthed into the world. Welcome to the motherhood club. Adjusting to a new schedule and routine with your baby is easier said than done. It's natural to have some worries that are harder to ease as a new mum. I'll address the most pressing that I've observed below.

Five Things New Mums Worry About but Shouldn't and How to Avoid Them.

1.   How you look. You're a new mum and you just had a baby! You're radiant, you're beautiful, so get rest and enjoy your new baby.

2.   The weight issue. Focus on the miracle in your arms not the extra weight you may or may not have gained. Spend time with your baby and family. You will have time to get back down to a healthy weight.

3.   Being everything to everyone! Stop taking on too much. Concentrate your efforts on you and your baby. Trying to be everything is only going to stress you out more. New mums that are on maternity leave try to do more because they are home. Don't run yourself ragged. Don't feel guilty for not doing anything. Get some help from mates and family. Now is not the time for being too proud to ask for support. I'll even give you permission that it's OK. When a mate asks if they can help just say 'yes'. If you have a husband or signif-icant other they should be picking up some of the slack. If your hubby/significant other is in the military like mine, he might not be there. That is the time to call on mates and relatives for help. Don't be scared to ask!

4.   Worrying about clothes. Don't worry about clothes. Put on your husband clothes. Wear a kaftan if you

want to. You are home, no one is seeing you. Spend time with your child and don't even worry about it. I promise the style advice is coming so keep reading!

5.   Hair issue. Lots of my mates worry about it. Are you guilty of this too? You go over to visit a mate who is a new mum and the first thing they say is "don't mind my hair". I'm like "Luv! You just had a baby no one is worried about your hair." Enjoy your family; don't stress yourself out so much about the little things. Even though I know that this is not what this book is about. However, I find that new mums over stress about their hair for no apparent reason. Let it go. Enjoy your first few moments of motherhood as much as possible. Make memories, they grow up fast!

6.   Have some luxury, go to the spa or get a at home spa kit. Sanctuary has some great ones that are reasonably priced.

Full Disclosure

This wasn't the best time for me style wise. I wasn't cute at all but I quickly learned what NOT to wear after giving birth. My body was different. Some women take longer to get back to pre-baby weight compared to others. Unfortunately, I was not one of the lucky ones to bounce back quickly. It took six months to return to my pre-baby weight. Even after all the working out and eating carefully my body was still very different from before. I had to dress according to my new physique if I wanted to still look fabulous.

Styling with Baby!

Nothing is where it used to be after you have a baby. The four to six weeks since your baby was born has passed. Now you are running around with baby in tow. Your body may still be changing as the pregnancy weight comes off. So what do you wear in the meantime?

The best style in my opinion and experience is Bohemian. Why? It's the easiest to wear.

The Bohemian look includes flowing maxi dresses, palazzo trousers, tops and tunics with leggings. It's a very figure friendly look. There is no structure in most of the garments, so they are flattering to the ever changing physique. A caveat to these looks is that once all the baby weight is gone the Bohemian style can integrate itself into your wardrobe.

Once your body is back to how it used to be (or as close at it is gonna get), you can add a belt or a little structure with accessories. These adjustments will work even for the size you are now. We will do a deep dive into getting your wardrobe where you want it in the coming chapters!

Looking Chic with Jr.

Looking chic with small children can be a cringe worthy ordeal. I learned this from personal experience. You want to look good. The challenge is styling yourself while knowing that, sooner or later, these tiny hands will grab onto a shirt or trousers and leave their mark. When you have small children, choose attire that is easy to wear – jeans, cute vests, things that you can wash and dry over and over and over again.

My answer to staying chic with children is to shop consignment. I still do so even to this day. It may not be glamorous and can be a bit time consuming, but it works. So, when Jr. wants to share his peanut butter and jelly sandwich with you or as my daughter says, "mummy give me a hug" with dirty hands from playing out back, I'm not pitching a fit.

When looking for designer pieces, the rule of thumb is to shop for quality. Not all high priced clothing are made to last. For example, I'm a big advocate of buying quality jeans because you could wear them for years. I'm not a fan of splurging on £ 1000 designer boots (regardless of how much I drool over them) or handbags made from material that easily breaks down in a year or two.

Always consider the long-term ROI (Return on Investment) before buying an expensive item. A great pair of denim never goes out of style. I have a pair of jeans from Express that I bought over six years ago! If you are going to spend that kind of money on certain items they need to last.

Inexpensive stores like Forever 21 is another great place to find £2 or £3 priced vests. This way if they get messed up you can throw them away or repurpose them. You can also invest a little more money in better quality vests that will maintain their shape through multiple washes and not fall apart on you. This is up to your budget and what you are comfortable with. You want fabrics that either are going to last or you do not mind having to repurpose.

Always be on the lookout. There are so many fabrics out there that are kid friendly and easy to clean. Any poly blend or rayon blend is really good. So is Jersey which is very, very figure friendly and easy to wash depending on the quality of the fabric. The higher the quality the greater the cost but these kinds of fabric are the best in child friendly clothing material in my experience. They are easily cleaned in the washing machine instead of needing to be dropped off at a dry cleaner.

Keep in mind no fabric is perfect. You should always have a

bleach pen and shout wipes with you at all times.

Pumps + Kids = Possible

A good mate of mine, Khaliha, phoned and asked me, "How do you wear pumps with children?" A new mum herself, Khaliha has a two-year-old and running after her in pumps was not working. What I told her was to invest in either some cute comfortable flats or kitten pumps until her daughter was older.

If you are a pump veteran like Rachel Zoe, and can run around in four and a half to six inch stilettos with your child, knock yourself out. I wore pumps prior to becoming pregnant and up until I was six months pregnant – but only on Sundays, really, because that's the only day I dressed up. Even now I wear pumps all of the time. It wasn't a hardship wearing pumps after pregnancy. I already knew the tricks of the trade.

For all the mums that want to wear fabulous boots here is what I suggest: Doctor your boots and feet. No matter how amazing those Manolo's look on you, if they blister your feet every time you wear them, what's the point of having them? Odds are, you will probably not wear them for very long. Let's be honest, pumps are not comfortable. Regardless of how much you pay for them they will not be perfect.

Everyone's foot is different. Some boots will rub your foot and cause blisters while others won't. Buy some moleskin or gel inserts for your pumps, it will make a world of difference. This is what they don't tell you about celebrities who wear those sky high stilettos. Moleskin can be cut into any shape that you need to put on the inside of your boots to stop rubbing against the skin. The gel inserts support the ball of your feet by adding more cushion that most pumps lack. Some inserts even come with arch support for those who need it or can be bought separately.

I strongly suggest, knowing your comfort level before buying a pair of stilettos. Yes, that means you have to go to the store and try several on! While in the store try BOTH shoes on and walk around. Why? Okay, true story! I bought a pair of shoes with one being the display shoe. Upon getting home found that I was given two different sizes and the display shoe was faded! Learn from my mistakes. You want to make sure they are not too high for you. This is not something you can judge with just one shoe on. If you are not used to wearing pumps, you can still wear them, its fine. Just remember it takes time to get used to walking around in stilettos that change your posture and gait.

My best advice on wearing pumps with children is to wait for one of two things – either your children are still in a stroller, or they're old enough that you don't have to chase after them.

Those pumps are not going to be comfortable for too long if you need to constantly chase a toddler. An alternative to pumps are wedges. Wedges are great if you want some height but more stability. Wedges come in differently heights and widths so again, try the pair on before walking out of the store with them.

If pumps are not your cup of tea then flats are it! There are some fabulous flats out there that are super comfortable, fashionable and available at various price ranges. For those of you looking for longevity and comfort, my go to pair are Coach and Cole Haan flats. The Coach flats already have the gel inserts in them and are designed for minor arch support. Coach flats, come in a variety of neutral colours that blend seamlessly into anyone's wardrobe. Cole Haan flats have Nike insoles to make them feel almost like trainers. I'm a big advocate of spending money on boots that are your daily drivers. These are the types of footwear that you wear most often because you will get your money's worth out of them.

The Survival Guide

When you are a stylish mum, there are some things that are just crucial to have in your purse. I learned this hard way so you can learn from my mistakes. These items will save the day!

Chocolate, ice cream, lolly pops, milkshakes, markers, crayons you name it, have happened to spill on me at one time or another to me. That is how I learned that a bleach pen is one of the items that are essential supplies in your purse if you're going to be a stylish mum on the town with kids.

Always carry a bleach pen, because it's either on your outfit or theirs. Along with the pen try to have Shout wipes with you, for stubborn or unexpected stains. Have moist wipes handy for your children as well as yourself.

Another essential item is a travel sewing kit. The little mini ones will do, nothing grandiose. Make sure the kit includes scissors because you never know. Case in point, I had a skirt rip because my daughter was on my hip and her foot got tangled in it when I tried to put her down. Yes, odd and not cute at all. We were not at home, so I went and bought a travel size sewing kit, whilst holding my skirt together. The patch work happened in the loo.

Keeping your style mojo is also about having plenty of high energy. Always carry a bottle of water and a snack with you. The best snacks are nuts, granola or dried fruit, because it really doesn't go bad. As mums our days get so busy we forget to eat. You just do. Between running after kids after you've gotten yourself ready, getting the kids ready, and out the door, you don't stop until well into your day. Often it's well past lunch before you remember that you didn't eat breakfast and lunch! Having snacks around are just what you need to keep your energy high. Energy boosting snacks are also good to keep you from losing your cool thanks to "hangry" (hungry + angry) attacks. Let's just say you're into a round of grocery shopping. Suddenly Junior decides to pitch a fit because you just walked past the fruit snacks. Well, if you whip out some granola or dried fruit, he's cool, at least for the next couple of minutes that it takes him to eat it.

Last, but not least, carry a mirror at all times. I know that sounds crazy, but when you're dealing with children, anything is liable to get on your face. It is always a good idea to double check. You never know. A lot of times you're so involved with what your kids are doing that you don't even pay attention to what you look like until you are in the store! That's my survival kit. I carry it even to this day. My kids are now aged 9 and 15 years respectively during the time of writing this book.

4: KNOW WHAT YOU HAVE

&

WORK IT!

You worked it before the kids came along. You can work it in your mummy years. Transitioning back into your pre-pregnancy clothing can be a hassle. You don't know what to wear. The figure you have now may be radically different from before baby. Your bust may be up a cup size or two or you have some "booty" where none existed before. There is nothing wrong with gaining or losing in these areas. You have new proportions and now let's learn to work with it!

Your style before becoming a mother may not match up with who you are now. Regardless of the reason, take a proactive approach to your wardrobe. It doesn't matter if you work at home or you go to the office every day. Our clothing and more importantly, our style, is a statement of who we are. The apparel we wear is a tangible representation of our personality. Don't be afraid to show your true colours. Never be afraid to be you. Let me show you a roadmap to bringing the real you to the world with a style uniquely your own.

Style Inspirations

Everyone has a style heroine. Some are famous icons like Diana Vreeland or Coco Chanel. Others are our mates or family only known to us. A style heroine can be a lifelong inspiration or for an era in our lives. We are all inspired and impacted by some form of style growing up. You may find yourself obsessed with a certain colour or article of clothing. Personally, I am a coveter of pencil skirts! There is a reason you love certain items. They align with your innate style.

The basic style inspirations are bohemian, classic, eclectic, and glamorous. Please note that these are just starting points. There are countless other styles to choose from such preppy, global, steam punk, and vintage. Many of the more distinct styles combine one or more of these style inspirations. Do not get hung up on trying to fit in a box. Remember, you are an original! These style categories are here to give you a starting point in developing your individual expression.

Examples of the style categories mentioned are:

Classic: Button-up shirts, jumper vests, blue denim, pea coats, sports blazers, khakis, and ankle or knee boots in neutral colours. Neutral colour palette. ***Designer:*** Ralph Lauren

Bohemian: Lace shirts, palazzo trousers, peasant tops, maxi dresses, fur vests, leather, fringe, earth tones, flower jewellery. ***Designer:*** Free People

Eclectic: Vibrant colours and patterns, mixing prints and textures to create a look that goes not necessarily matching. ***Designer:*** Betsy Johnson

Glamorous: Fine fabrics like silk, cashmere, and satins. Fur coats and ball gowns. Over the top chunky jewellery. ***Designer:*** Oscar De La Renta

How Do You Choose Your Style?

What speaks to you? Don't think about it. The answers that quickly come to mind – that's your style! The trick is to assemble items that peak your fancy in to an ensemble that flatters you. If you love flowing maxi dresses, beautiful prints and lace you might be a Boho chick. Does Ralph Lauren's collections catch your eye because you like clean lines, crisp trousers, and well-tailored jackets? If so, you may be more of a classic girl. Is it natural for you to throw on a plaid shirt, leather trousers and metallic sky-high pumps? Eclectic is your innate style.

Some people are very traditional but have romantic Bohemian qualities to their clothing. You don't have to stay with that clothing or with that style. For example, Madonna went from a street urchin look in 1984 to her current incarnation with various styles in between. As you evolve the message your style sends out a message of who you are. Personal style can be a form of expressing what inspires you. Play with some ideas.

Browse through fashion magazines or websites to brainstorm what your look will be like. For instance, you might wear trouser denim trousers (classic) with a sheer floral top (bohemian) and chunky jewellery (glamorous) and it will all work together.

Mixing your style is the fun part. So what draws you? You could be a stay-at-home mum that is very Bohemian with cowboy boots, floral dresses, and jean jackets. That look works and you can intertwine other styles with it. For example, add some glamour with accessories. This is just a basis to start from.

For the mums who are reading this that are confused, or are thinking, "Well, I like all three," or, "I like two of them," that's fine. This is about inspiration, not following a set of rigid rules. There is no "fashion law" that decrees that you have to dress this way. Everything here is to give you a foundation and from there, you can expound and make it your own style. My goal is to give you the steps to create your own look that you love!

The Body Types

Just like there are style types there are also body types. Style is about maximizing your best assets. How I style one body shape will differ from another. This is why duplicating someone else never fully works especially if they have a very different type of body than you. If you are inspired by a celebrity or fashion icon it's important to adjust their style strategy to your shape. Otherwise you may be setting yourself up for frustration. The basic body types are as follows:

Pear: You are bigger on the bottom than you are on the top.

That just means your measurements for your bust to waist ratio are not proportionate to your waist and hips. Your waist to your hip ratio is going to be bigger. ***Celebrity example:*** Beyoncé.

Square: There is really no difference between the waist and the hips. Usually, in a square shape body there is less than a two inch difference between your bust, your waist and your hips. ***Celebrity Example:*** Cameron Diaz, Jordan Dunn.

Apple: Your bust and waist measurements have a bigger difference between them compared to your waist to hip ratio. Proportionally you are top heavy. ***Celebrity Example:*** Angelina Jolie.

Hourglass: Your bust is proportioned to your hips. ***Celebrity Example:*** Halle Berry, Scarlett Johansson.

Now you know what those basic body types mean. None of them are bad. One is not better than another. Just work with what you have and accentuate what you love. Some women who are apples and very busty can't stand the fact that they're top heavy. They want to hide their bust. Then you have some apples that love having ample cleavage, so much they show it off as much as possible. Identify your type, know how to work it, and remember that a seamstress is your best mate but also keep a tailor on speed dial when out shopping.

Style Your Body Type

"Give me an example of the best styles – like one style for each body type."

Pear: I love pear-shaped in vintage dresses. The ones with portrait collars, a tucked- in waist, and a full A-line skirt. To me, it's gorgeous and ultra-elegant. For a modern-day look on a pear-shape, I'd probably style her in a patterned or a floral striped top with a high-waisted wide legged black pant. This is a very professional look. Next, I would add a pair of pumps to give her some height and elongate her. The black pant will also lengthen her appearance from her torso all of the way down to her feet and minimize her hips while balancing her top and bottom. For a more casual look an empire waisted sundress is a go to item.

Square: Baby doll dresses are so cute on square shaped ladies. If I were to style with separates, it would be really cute shorts, but not too short, or the high-waisted shorts, and a really cute peasant top. This look would be an easy every day look. Other possibilities are a striped tunic belted at the waist with skinny jeans and some cute flats. We belt the top to create the appearance of a waist to balance your top and bottom.

Apple: For an apple shape, I would probably style with a wrap shirt in a solid colour with a print patterned pencil skirt to off-set and draw more attention away from your chest and towards her lower body. This look will balance out proportions. Another look for everyday would be a V-neck tee shirt in a neutral solid colour, trouser denim and kitten pumps. This look can be layered upon with scarves, blazers and jewellery to give you either a casual feel or more dressy.

Hourglass: A wrap dress all the way. It's most flattering look on an hourglass. Another excellent style for this figure is a body con dress with a belt if the body con dress is an all over pattern. These beauties also look fabulous in high waist wide legged jeans and a simple tee shirt. Yes, I know simple right?

Why Pick A Style?

You pick a style just so you have a foundation to build from. Once you have your style foundation the rest is you. Remember, true style is about who you are, not fashion trends or fads. It's who you are. When you put on clothes and go out in the world, your style represents who you are to people without speaking.

Style is an unspoken powerful personal statement. Consider what impression you give off if you were to walk down the street dressed as any of the following: punk rocker, biker chick, hippie, high fashion posh like Victoria Beckham, surfer girl casual, or corporate suite. Now think what message each one of those looks would convey to people. Who would approach you? Who would not? Why?

So what do you want people to know about you? Do you want to go out and say, *"I'm a Sex and the City gal"* by wearing Carrie Bradshaw inspired attire? Imagine someone walking around wearing cigarette trousers, a cute little shirt, belt, and a pair of high pumps. Now consider what message that look broadcasts. Will someone see you and think, "Okay, she's confident. I really like that" or "She's well put together."

Your style is just your guidepost. It's what you're going to fall back on when you don't know what to do. Now do not think that you should be over worried about what people think. That is not what I am trying to convey. I want you to make sure you are showing the world who you are. Your personality via clothing.

If you're reading this and think "I really don't have a style," or "I can't pick one," then look at what's in your wardrobe. Do you have a lot of traditional items? Do you have a lot of colour? Do you have a lot of patterned items? Do you have a lot of stuff that doesn't match? Go from there. Usually if you have a lot of traditional items, you probably have a traditional style. Do you not have a lot of eccentric clothing and or is your clothing very conservative? Traditional is likely your natural style.

Again, this is just a starting point it helps you navigate fashion choices better. Knowing your style helps avoid getting sucked into buying trendy clothing that won't flatter you. Having a style foundation is like a lighthouse that keeps you away from the dangers of Daisy Dukes and see-through outfits. Yep, I said that!

How to Add Trends to A Wardrobe/Style On A Budget

Relax. The myth of needing a 6 figure budget to stay in style is just that – a myth!   Once you have the foundations in your wardrobe, you can start adding items that speak to you and bring out your best assets.

For instance, let's just go back to the basic white button-down and a pair of skinny jeans scenario. So, say that the biggest trend out right now are turban style headpieces and you LOVE them. How do you add them into your wardrobe? If you want to start small then just wear a colourful or neutral one with said white button down and skinny jeans. If you are more adventurous try adding statement jewellery pieces with the look. Feeling like having some fun? Wear a colourful turban with a tribal pat-terned dress!

Let's say Bollywood is a trend. You have a button-down shirt and some skinny jeans. How do you insert Bollywood into your style? So accessorize! You can go the turban route by using a beautifully patterned scarf to create a turban. Wear beautiful jewel toned necklace, rings or shoes using a gold belt to finish look.

There are little ways to add trends on a budget. Sometimes there is no need to spend money at all. Just do your makeup heavier and with highly pigmented eyeshadows or liners on the eyes. Henna tattoos are an easy add and are not permanent.

Mums on a budget have ways to insert trendy items without spending a lot of money. Thrift stores have many inexpensive treasures. So do consignment shops and yard sales. For online shoppers, always search on eBay and Etsy to find who is selling what. Researching the culture behind a trend on the Internet can lead you to some authentic places where you can buy items on a bargain.

If you have a rock and roll style, like myself, you can insert your love of rock and roll in vests. You will also find an AC/DC shirt in my wardrobe that I love to wear. I've worn it with a cute skirt and a blazer. You can take something as simple as a leather wrap bracelet and add that little bit of edge to your look. However,

I'm not going out with the cut up jeans and spiked leather jacket wearing a bandana around my head. My rocker chic is about embracing a trend or style by making it my own. Any other way would render me a clone and I'm original to the core!

Trends are cute. They're fun. Fads are even more outrageous sometimes. The whole point of having a personal style is that it will make you shine. Adding trendy clothing is about accentuating it rather than replacing the style you already have. If there is a trend that you like, find a way to incorporate it. Make it your own. Who wants to look like another person? You don't want to appear to be somebody you are not. That's why we have our individual personal styles.

5 Ways to Put Outfits Together Effortlessly: Don't overthink. Do it on instinct

First, you have your own style. Second, you know what you like and don't like. Here is what I do. Let's say it's Sunday and I'm planning for the rest of my week. I would pull out five things that I love. So I go in to my wardrobe and pull out five articles of clothing. It doesn't matter what they are. It could be five shirts, three shirts, two skirts, and my favourite pair of stiletto pumps. Or it could be two skirts and three dresses. The specific items don't matter because you just pull out the five things you love and we go from there.

The five items are simply five things that you love and want to wear this week. The first one could be a shirt. If that's your first pick the next step is to ask yourself what trousers you are going to wear. Then just go down the line. It's the quickest and most efficient way. Don't overthink. Do it on instinct. When you're done selecting your five items just walk away. Really. Just leave them out and walk away. Wait a few hours and come back to look at your selection. Now you have another chance to look at your choices with fresh eyes.

Don't overthink when reviewing your selection. Just look at each piece and say, "Yes. Yes, that works." If something doesn't work, brainstorm ideas about what will make it work. Say you have a top and bottom, and you're thinking, "Ugh, I'm really not feeling that." So ask yourself why you aren't feeling it. Does it need a belt? Does it need accessories? Do you need to pick out the right boots? Do you just need to try it on? That's where you would go more in depth.

I promise you that if you just go with your gut and pull five out-fits out, walk away and come back versus of standing there and being like, "Oh, do I really like this?" you will make styling yourself for the week much easier. If you don't second guess yourself everything will be fine, because you have a style.

5 Ways to Dress Down and Still Look Chic

Truthfully, enjoy dressing down. Some people think my dressing down is not really dressing down. I just take it as my casual chic is better than average! Just because you are dressing down doesn't mean you can't be cute. Here are some ideas:

Joggers: joggers are a great way to dress down and still look cute. Throw on a pair of printed joggers and you're done. Printed joggers, a cute vest, sandals or pumps, and voila! Even in tennis boots, you're done.

Shirt dresses: I love them! Throw one on, wear flip-flops, add a belt, etc. You can wear them in so many ways. Put on Gladiator sandals, throw on combat boots if you want to, and they are cute. Graphic Shirt dresses especially are so much fun!

Ripped jeans: I love these too! When you dress down in a nice pair of ripped up jeans, throw on a pair of red pumps, and watch out! It doesn't matter how you put it together it works with everything. They can be worn with boots, flats, and tennis shoes go right ahead. Mix with a graphic vest and you're dressed down but still ready for after 5. Top the look off with a leather motto jacket and your ready for cocktails or date night.

A-line skirts: Similar to a skater's skirt and worn with a jumper equals done. Pair it with flats or a pair of boots and you're ready to go out the door in style in no time. You're dressed down but still smashingly cute.

Maxi dress: Of course the maxi dress. Everybody needs maxi dresses in their life. You take a maxi dress. Wear a pashmina around your neck and keep it moving with some flip-flops or some gladiator sandals, and pronto, you're ready to roll. Put a blazer over it and it completes the look. A maxi dress is instant dress-down chic.

STYLISH MUM: A STYLE PRO-FILE CHECKLIST

Always review your style profile checklist before you start planning your next shopping trip. Planning is pivotal in building your personal brand of style.

Body Type	
Favourite Examples of Style with Your Body Type	
Style Inspirations for Your Body Type (i.e. Classic)	
What Event are you shopping for? (Brunch, Black tie, vacation)	
What do you want to find?	
What is your Budget?	
Where are you going? Do they have a sale coming up? Check the website for deals before you go!	

This handy sheet will help you stay focused while shopping!

5: STYLE IN PIECES

Any woman, mum or not, must have certain essentials in their wardrobe: A three-piece black suit with a jacket, skirt and/or trousers. A pair of comfortable black pumps in either leather or patent. A pair of jeans. Now I know you are probably thinking, "Oh, yeah, everybody has a pair of jeans." What I am talking about is, "Jeans that make you feel like a rock star!" These are jeans that you can wear out with mates, at the office on casual days, or on the weekend. Always have two or three pairs of these jeans. Make sure they are cut for your body. Have them hemmed for your pump height and tailored to your shape.

Next "must have" item are casual trousers. I'm talking about a pair of chinos or trousers that you can wear dressed up down. These will be in addition to the suit trousers I mentioned earlier.

Don't you dare forget to include a little black dress (otherwise known as the LBD) in your wardrobe! Every woman needs to have one. An LBD is an investment piece. I'll say more about that later in this chapter. Every woman also needs a nice white shirt, button up or a blouse. I tell all of my clients, "You need to have this only because you can wear it open, closed, to work, or out for drinks." Same advice goes for the pencil skirt. You already have one skirt with your suit but you also need a patterned one. That livens things up. Any pattern you like will do.

Pick polka dot, striped, floral, or the comic book ones which I find are super cute since I love DC and Marvel comic books. Style requires at least a little bit of that diversity in your wardrobe. This is a piece that you can always come back to and dress up and down.

Notice the theme here: the dress up, dress down strategy. Having foundational pieces in your closet are the keys to doing so. Always have them in your wardrobe. No excuses.

And there's more!

You're also going to need an A-line skirt that looks great on everybody. Now the length of the A-line skirt is what's going to get you. Make sure it is appropriate for your height. For the petite ladies like myself (5'1"), the A-line skirts are either 2 inches above or below the knee. One of the more popular lengths is midi-length. This elongates your legs and makes you calves appear shapelier.

Now if you're 5'9", I do not recommend you wear really, really short skirts. Watch out for that temptation. It is a lot harder for tall ladies to find a skirt compared to me. Being statuesque you can probably do two or three inches above your knee or at your knee. Either option looks really good on tall women anyway.

A trench coat is another must have. Yes, it is very classic. It spans decades, from the film era that brought us *"Casablanca"* up to today. Find one that speaks to you. They tend to come in caramels and creams, but you can easily find them in bright patterns and prints.

The leather jacket. One that behaves like a Moto jacket. They too come in various shapes, lengths, patterns and colours. Again, get a piece that speaks to you and one you will wear year round. Don't go for the bright yellow with green flowers that is costly unless you are going to wear it longer than a season. If you want a caramel one, go right ahead. This is an investment piece of good quality leather which will last you a lifetime, so choose wisely. Biker-style jackets are an option for your leather foundational piece. These do not go out of style. James Dean put them on the map and they are not going anywhere. Shop around and invest the time to find these foundational pieces. Remember to buy things that you love as well as need in the best quality you can afford.

The Day dress or wrap dress. Think Diane von Furstenberg. Wrap dresses look amazing on on all figures but is the go-to dress for all my hourglass ladies. You can get wrap dresses that have an A-line skirt which works wonders for my pear shaped ladies and those who want to conceal more on the bottom.

Wrap dress for the straight body type can have pin tuck cap sleeves or detailing at the shoulder and some detailing at the bottom. Apple shapes depending on your comfort level can wear a wrap dress with a A-Line, straight or luminous skirt. The top can be plain or detailed. Want to show some more of your figure? Get one that has a straight skirt.

A pair of black or coloured wide-legged trousers should also be on the list. These are classics that go with almost all the body shapes. Make sure these trousers are hemmed to the floor while you are in pumps to elongate your figure.

Skirts for Your Occasions

I love skirts! Every woman should have an A-line skirt and a pencil skirt. Depending on your lifestyle and what you do every day, that determines the kind of skirt to have in your wardrobe. One of my clients is a stay-at-home mum. A lot of her attire is very flowy. This includes jersey maxi dresses and maxi skirts. She also has cute yoga and jersey skater skirts that might hit at her knee. All those looks work for her.

Another client is a career mum who has pencil skirts and longer A-line skirts for the office, all those are fine. A-line skirts work with all body types. If you put it on the smaller part of your waist (natural waist) it accentuates it while making it look even smaller! Ladies with a long torso can do this to define their waist. The same goes for hourglass vixens. You can also include a fuller skirt that goes midi length if you are not keen on maxi skirts.

Formal Clothing

Only if you attend formal events should you have formal dresses ready to wear in your wardrobe. Women who have a lot of formal occasions to attend and have the money, yes, invest in formal dresses. Don't go out and start buying formal dresses unless you just lucked up on a Jason Wu original for £ 20. If you do, call me. I'll take it off your hands.

Little Black Dresses (LBD) are great for dates, and yes, we mums still date. We date our husbands, our number one men and the occasional girls' night out! Couples do still date and socialize with mates. We go to Christmas parties and social engagements. The LBD is perfect for all those occasions. Find a very classic one, like a sheath or skater dress and throw a belt on with it one year but next year wear it with a cute little patterned bolero. Or put a colourful shirt under it another year. No one would know that it's the same dress, really. Trust me, they won't.

Foundational Pieces Must Haves

When I say foundation pieces in this context then it means not staple pieces but what you wear under these clothes. These set the stage for garments to drape correctly over your frame. Every woman should own Spanx or some kind of shaper especially us mums. It has nothing to do with whether you're in shape, have a flat stomach, or carry the curves of a mum. Wearing shape-wear has to do with how fabric flows. A swankier dress, like a wrap or body-con, will fit better with foundational pieces like Spanx. This type of shaper eliminates visible panty lines and allows the dress to flow over the body. No one is going to tell you that you have visible panty lines, unless you walk past me and ask me how you look, because that is what a friend would do, right?

A nice smooth appearance ensures that people see you. Not your visible panty lines, puckers, or bulges. Foundational clothing is exactly that. Clothes can lay on you the way it's supposed to. Shapers are available in full body, which includes the bra shaper. Or you can get a skirt shaper and a waist clincher. Whichever you're more comfortable with. I personally like the shorts that pull up under your bra, they act as a belly slimmer (my problem area). Get the best of both worlds.

The Bra Issue

Did you know that most of us walk around wearing the wrong bra? A bra will make or break an outfit, period. A bra that does not fit will make your girls look like they're two inches lower. Or you look like the owner of the infamous mono boob. I'm fine with cleavage. Every woman should not fear showing a proper level of cleavage. Come on that is one of the best things about being a woman!

For all ladies, a great bra can't be underestimated as an essential foundation piece. Avoid mistakes before you buy one. I personally recommend going to a place where you will be measured accurately.

The number one bra every woman should have is a vest bra. Depending on the size of your bust (C cup or larger) you will need an underwire. A t-shirt bra is seamless. You won't have any lines when worn with vests and other fitted shirts.
Women need a bra in their wardrobe that fits the types of shirts they wear often. If you wear V-necks, a plunge bra may work better than a full coverage bra. For strapless dresses or shirts, wear a strapless bra or bandeau.

The number one piece of advice from me on bra shopping: Shop at Bravissimo, Dillard's, or Nordstrom, to be properly fitted. Not to bash Victoria's Secret or anything but they don't carry all sizes. I'm confident that when I go to Nordstrom or Bravissimo, I will be sized correctly. These stores have a wider range of sizes for your girls.

Underwire bras are a necessity in life and are comfortable when wearing your correct size. A high quality bra is one of the best investments for your lingerie collection. As expensive as bras are, a good quality one will last through washing and drying that sucker for years. That's just the way it is. A cheap bra falls apart after the third wash. Don't get me started about some tragic experiences with bras it is too sad.

A bra that fits all of your situations is imperative. If you have this beautiful gown with a very deep V-neck, there is a bra for that. Don't think that Angelina Jolie doesn't wear a bra. She does. Trust me. None of these stars leave home without wearing them underneath their attire. They all do. If all else fails, the bras are sewn into their dresses. As any of my fashion queens will know, bras, knickers, everything can be sewn into these dresses and other formalwear. So all you have to do is just put your birthday suit in there. I don't care if you're an A-cup all of the way up to a G. You need a good bra.

STYLE PIECES WORKHEETS

Wardrobe Audit: Create a checklist of the contents of your wardrobe. Based on the foundation pieces mentioned in this chapter, create a list of items you still need. This will help make shopping trips more effective.

Foundational Items	Items You Already Have	Items Still Needed
Jeans		
A-line Skirts (solid and patterned)		
Pencil Skirts (solid and patterned)		
LBD		
Trench coat		
Leather Jackets		
Day dresses		
Wrap dresses		
Formal clothing		
Bras (By Type)		
Shapewear (By Type)		
White Button up shirt		

Measuring Up: Know your measurements. Just because you found a dream outfit, don't buy it unless it suits your dimensions. If you purchase an item that needs to be altered, this checklist will be handy.

Height	
Bust size/Cup size	
Waist	
Hips	
Torso Length	
Leg Length	
Arm Length	
Shoe Size	

6: FINDING THE TIME TO BE STYLISH

Time is the most precious resource. When it comes to styling your time is precious. Many organizational experts say that time planning is really life planning. I call it style timing. Like with anything else, putting time in the beginning to plan, makes life so much easier towards the end. Styling is strategic. If you put the time in on whatever day works for you to map out your style for the week, you'll be amazed how runway ready can be quick and fast every day. The simple formula is plan it out, get every-thing together in advance for the week, and breeze through the next seven days in style.

Mums especially are pressed for time every second of the day. Style timing is about grace under pressure. You don't stress about it. You don't wake up saying, "What am I going to wear?" because it's already picked out. I know that's one of those "duh" things. Our mums made us pick out our outfits for school the night before.

There's a reason that my mum or grandma would insist, "Toya, get your stuff out for tomorrow. Iron it. Get it ready. So in the morning you're not scrambling." Of course we always say, "I won't be scrambling." Wrong! Of course when I woke up in the morning, I was scrambling! For those who aren't morning peo-ple, this hazardous routine ruins many a morning.

What's the first step in style timing? It begins with the right foundation. By having the right things in your wardrobe you can style time in no time. Let me take you through how I plan my mornings.

Morning Beauty Hacks –
Time Savers without Compromising Style

Having kids limits your morning prep time. You still want to look your best but you don't have a whole lot of time to really spend on getting ready. Get up before your kids. I know this is a tough one, but if you get up before them and get yourself ready then you are done. Plus, you will have some quiet time to yourself. It took me a while to learn this. I still wanted to do full on makeup with lashes after my mummy years started. It can be done. I'm just not able to be human until after my second cup of coffee in the morning. Until then it's even harder to focus on applying lashes.

Trying to do it all with kids in tow was making me crazy, just for the sake of makeup. I love make-up but I'm not a makeup artist. Rather, I'm more like a make-up artist wannabe.

When supermodel Tyra Banks was promoting the five-minute face, it made me think, "What can I do in five minutes that gives me the look I want? Something that I can keep together for the rest of the day. Something that's nice, not over the top, but still looks good, and doesn't suck 45 minutes out of my life every morning?" So, I dialed down my morning beauty regime and was pleasantly surprised. Here they are in order:

Eyes: When I realized that you do your eyes _BEFORE_ applying foundation, WOW! What a difference it made! On occasion I use concealer or an eye shadow primer but not every day. Apply eyeliner to the eyes then two coats of mascara on eyelashes. Starting with the eyes means that any make-up mistakes can be easily fixed without having to worry about reapplying foundation!

Brows & Concealer: Start with your eyebrows. This includes anything that needs concealer on my face because I use concealer to shape my brows. _Disclaimer:_ This will take some practice to do quickly. Try to give yourself a few extra minutes to get the hang of it. Practice on a weekend when you have spare time to master the art of shaping brows and applying concealer.

Face: Get yourself a beauty balm (BB) and colour corrector (CC) cream or a good tinted moisturizer to wear. This can be applied with your fingers or brushes. Try putting it on with your fingers first. Then use a stipple brush to blend, blend, and blend! Next, brush on some powder to set the look and you are almost done. If you do blush, add that here!

Lips: Use a lip liner on your mouth first then apply lipstick. This helps keep the colour on your lips last longer. Keep the same tube of lipstick in your purse just in case. Follow these five steps and it's all the makeup you need to take with you!

Setting: So it will last all day try a setting spray. Some are rose water, Urban Decay's All Nighter or SmashBox Photo Finish Primer Water to name a few.

This truly is all I do before dashing out the door! I only recently added the BB/CC creams to my morning makeup routine after a mate showed me how in a Sephora store. You can also add lashes or contouring to this list. The five steps gives you a great baseline to draw from.

Advanced Beauty Hacking

There are so many time saving make-up products out there. Eyebrow and concealer creams are some of my newest beauty products and I love them! BB cream stands for beauty balm, they come tinted and transparent. CC creams stand for Colour Correction creams and are ideal for people who have redness or unevenness to their skin tone.

Both of these products can come with SPF, primer, anti-aging properties, moisture, blemish control, and many more. Having all these properties saves you time and money. You don't have to buy all these different products and apply them separately. If you want to put foundation over the top of the creams, you're more than welcome to, because it has a primer in it. It's just like a one-step. You can use them instead of foundation.

For dark circles under the eyes, try to get at least six hours of sleep and drink plenty of water. Then find a great under eye cream. My personal favourite is by Dr. Organics with Rose oil. If I do pull an all-nighter, I will most likely go the concealer route to hide those tired bags under my eyes. Using more concealer can be a time drain, so try concealer sticks. Brushes are not necessary, just use your ring finger to blend.

Hair Hacks

Hair can be a touchy subject for some. Not for me! I am a "do what you want with it" type person. It is in fact YOUR hair. After you have kids you want to look your best without having to dedicate an hour to do your hair. Time is precious so pick a hair style that you love but has minimal prep time.

For example, when I was pregnant with my daughter, my hair was roughly 13 inches long. Towards the end of my pregnancy it was a very hot summer. Not only could I not stand for a long period of time but I got tired very quickly. Styling my hair like before was nearly impossible. I couldn't put a relaxer in it. So I had the thought, "You know what? I'll just cut it all off." It wasn't the first time and wouldn't be the last time I decided to do the big chop. Once these locks were gone it was easier to maintain for the rest of my pregnancy and after childbirth.

Now I hear some of you already saying, "Are you crazy? I would have just gone and gotten it done, or do it up in a ponytail." That might work for you but for me cutting it off just made my life easier. My point is, I do not want you stressing about your hair and wasting time with it. If you have really long hair and you feel good to throw it up in a topknot, go for it!

Whatever works for you is key. As long as you're confident in how you look walking out the door that's all that matters. If it takes you five minutes to get it up there, then do it.

On the other hand, if you have long hair and dreading it, or you hate it then…cut it off. Yes, go right ahead. I'm giving you permission. I am all for the snip, snip! It's just easier. Shorter hair is easier to maintain. It's easier to work with. If you have curly hair like myself, when you cut it short, you get a look that has spanned the ages from the 1930s to modern day natural. You can just get it wet in the morning, walk out the door and keep it moving.

If you have chin-length hair with a natural curl consider letting it go curly in the morning. Its time consuming to blow dry and flat iron it before getting the kids ready for school. Give yourself a break. Besides, I'm pretty sure it looks really good curly. Try it and see!

When you're expecting and/or a new mum this is the time for finding a new cut and a style that is easy to maintain. Talk with your hair stylist. Find a hairdo that is easy. This is one of those haircuts that's going to look good with just a wash and go or looks good with only five minutes of styling.

Low maintenance hair doesn't mean a downgrade in fabulous. Master cutters and master stylists are the best resources to help you find an easy to upkeep cut and style that complements your face shape and personality.

One of my biggest pet peeves is people defining you by your hair. Your hairstyle is an expression of you. You have options! Don't believe you don't! If you talk to a stylist and they don't give you good enough options, go to another, and another, or go online and look at pictures and find a look. First, search for pictures. Second, find a stylists in your area that can do them. Third, schedule a consultation and talk to these stylists. Make sure you find out what is involved in maintaining the new do you have in mind.

You don't want to go and get the cutest pixie cut and find out that you need A, B, C, D, and E products in order to keep up with the look. Or you want to have this big, beautiful Beyoncé hair, but you have to follow an elaborate routine for it before going to bed. You have to curl it, wrap it, and then when you get up in the morning, you've got to take it all out. No, you find a different style. Unless you have beauty crew like Beyoncé, most people have no time for all of that.

For my ladies who love wigs, I'm there with you. I love a good wig. Lace fronts are the most natural with human hair that you can curl, wash, dry and dye. Before buying a wig make sure you measure your head to get the right size. The greatest part of wearing wigs…no maintenance! You just take it off and when ready put it back on. For the ladies who have weaves, make sure you get hair that is minimal maintenance. One client of mine did nothing but sew-ins during her pregnancy. She just didn't have the time so it worked for her. It does not work for everybody. Be truthful with yourself and ask how much primping are you willing and able to do in the mornings? Will this hairstyle fit into that time you have available? Always know what works for you or else you won't feel confident and it will cramp your style. Whatever has minimum maintenance and you feel good with, you need to go with that.

7: TRENDS, JEWELLERY, & LINGERIE

To Be or Not to Be … Trendy

If you are reading this book and cleaning out your wardrobe, trendy pieces are not for you… yet. You want to make sure that you have everything you need from day-to-day. You want to develop your style first. Then we'll talk about trendy pieces.

If you already have an established style, you're just reading to see what I'm talking about (which I thank you for!). You're ready to invest in trendy pieces. Just make sure they work for your style. If it doesn't work for you then, there is no point in following or spending money on the trend.

Got Jewellery?

Now there are some style tips and tactics around jewellery that I'm actually going to go over with in "What are the Ten Accessories that Every Woman Should Have?" There are some accessories and jewellery pieces that every woman should have. I'm just going to count those down:

Hoops. Every woman needs a pair of hoop earrings. I don't care if they are gold, silver, platinum, diamond hoops, whatever. Every woman needs a pair of hoops because they work with many occasions – pretty much almost all of them! Plus they are just easy to throw on. Hoops go from every day to night, to the weekends, and to work. You can wear hoops anytime.

Diamond Solitaires. I'm an advocate for diamond solitaires. They too work with everything. It's minimalistic elegance with solitaire diamond earrings.

Meaningful Pendant. Every woman should have a pendant that you feel strongly about. Your style is your personality made tangible, plus it draws the eye to your collar bone and elongates the neck!

Bracelet. Every woman should have a bracelet that they love, such as a chain or bangle bracelet. Not so much something gaudy, or something expensive, just a bracelet that you feel good putting on. It's simple enough to wear every day, and still elegant and small enough that it's not going to get in the way if you decide to add more to it. Makes sense?

Leopard Scarf. I know that's kind of off, but it is what it is. Every woman should have a leopard scarf, period. End of discussion. I promise. Leopard is a staple in every woman's wardrobe. I am an advocate of leopard and all animal prints therein. Animal prints like leopards are considered neutrals and easily spice up an outfit.

Black Purse. One you can carry everything you may ever need in. A nice, 12 X 12 piece that is almost like a briefcase, but a really cute purse. Tory Birch and Michael Kors design some really great ones. I also recommend a lovely tote purse for business or weekend trips. One that does double duty and is big enough to hold a pair of pumps.

If you go shopping, you can look cute in the beginning, but when your feet start hurting, you want to make sure you have a pair of flats in there.

Leopard Flats. Leopard print is a neutral. It works. Throw on a pair of leopard flats with a pair of jeans and a white button-up. Voila! You are automatically channelling Audrey Hepburn. Traditional and so classic. Dressed to the nines without trying.

Red Shoes. Whether a pair of flats, mules, pumps, or boots, there is just something about red shoes that are attention grabbers. Red shoes add interest to any outfit. One moment you are wearing just a regular black dress but throw on some red flats and its instant chic.

A White Blazer. I know that seems kind of unconventional, especially if you're a mum. Trust me. It's all good. Get a cream blazer if white makes you cringe. Just get that blazer. A white blazer brightens your whole outfit and is refreshing. Put it on with a pink shirt, over some jeans or the top of a cute dress, and you're glowing with a springy look. Don't worry about the rules of when you can and can't wear white. A white or cream blazer is appropriate at all times and during all seasons.

Sunglasses. I love sunglasses. You have to have sunglasses. Find a pair that complements your face shape. Invest in sunglasses that protect your eyes and protect them like your life depended on it. I enjoy looking posh behind a pair of sunglasses when I'm style stalking in the city. Sunglasses are like instant makeup. You can just put on lipstick and not do anything else on your eyes that day if you wear sunglasses everywhere.

Now that we have gone over style, body type, taken everything out of your wardrobe that doesn't look good on you in the first place, bought your foundational pieces, your outfit should work. Pretty much everything in your wardrobe should go together if you have the right style foundation.

Mistakes to Avoid when Buying a Bra

1. The first of the five mistakes women make when buying bras are that they buy them too little.
2. Number two is that they buy bras that are too big, and

they do go for those because they don't know what a real bra feels like [laughs], or they don't know what their real size looks like.

3. Buying bras at department stores. I'm not knocking you all with the department store bra, but if you're going to go to a department store, Wal-Mart is not it. You need to go to a Dillard's or a Lord & Taylor – someplace where they send their people away to learn how to measure you. It is imperative that you go and get a real bra.

4. Women, when they buy bras, do not hook the back of their bra on the last hook. They hook it on the tightest hook. You never do that. A bra will stretch out. It will not stretch in, so you always buy a bra that fits perfectly on the last one.

5. Another mistake I see often, and let me go back to my observations that women don't try clothes on over the top of their bras when they buy them. I don't know why, but you have got to try your clothes on. Put a shirt on over the top of your bra when you are trying it on so that you can see what your girls look like. You know it fits. Make sure you're not pouring out the top of it. Make sure, if it's supposed to be a Vest bra, that it's seamless. If it's supposed to be a push-up bra, make sure your girls are pushed up. You're not going to be able to tell if you just look at yourself in the mirror. Put on a

shirt. Once you put that shirt on over it, it gives you a different perspective.

These five tips should cover all of the ways you can avoid it. Go to a place where the associates are trained to measure you. Try your clothes on with your bra. Make sure you know your size and try different brands of bras. Don't go into a place and try one brand out of the eight they may have. Every brand cuts their bras a different way, so try, try, try your bras on.

THE STYLISH MUM JEWELLERY CHECKLIST

Apart from insurance purposes, it's also a good idea to keep track of the contents of your jewellery box. Knowing what you have already will help you identify the items you still need to add.

Items	Quantity/Description
Hoops	
Diamond Solitaires	
Pendants	
Bracelet	
Leopard Scarfs	
Black Purse	
Leopard Flats	
Red Boots	
White Blazer	
Sunglasses	

8: SHOP TO INVEST IN STYLE

What Are the Six Things Women Don't Do Before Going Shopping?

Number One

First of all, most women go shopping without knowing what is in their wardrobe. That is **numero uno!**

Number Two

Since they don't know what's in their wardrobe, they will buy something that doesn't go with anything in their wardrobe or nothing at all!

Number Three

Women make emotional purchases not strategic style selections. Once home their reaction to their purchases are, "Why did I buy this?"

Number Four

Shopping without a plan. Not knowing what is needed in their wardrobe makes women not think before buying. They don't know if they actually need a white shirt. Their approach is to just say, "Oh, I need a white shirt" not "What kind of white shirt do I need? What event is it for? Why am I shopping for it?" We would save a lot of money as women if we knew what we were going to shop for before we left the house.

Number Five

Shopping with the wrong people. When I go shopping with a client the clothing in their shopping bags are a lot different and everything enhances the style power of their wardrobe. Most women go shopping with mates or their kids with them. Mates love you so they will say "You look Fab in that". In real life you should have got that outfit in a different colour. Shopping with kids may allow us to spend more time with them but it's not ideal. Potty and snack breaks interrupt shopping and makes the experience so stressful we sometimes just buy an item because we are stressed and need something to wear.

Number Six

Wearing the wrong undergarments while shopping. This makes trying on outfits challenging. Why? The wrong bra doesn't allow you to see the best form or fit in the clothes you try on. If you are going to look for a strapless dress don't wear or bring a regular vest bra to the store. Wear a strapless one to get an idea of how the dress truly looks on you!

What Are Investment Pieces?

Investment pieces are either foundation pieces of your

wardrobe, special occasion items, or things that you fall in love with that you just can't live without. Even if you only wear it once a year, it doesn't matter. You love it. Think a Coach Purse, a tailored suit, or Dolce & Gabbana LBD that is just perfection and never goes out of style. Investment pieces are timeless. That is the big thing to remember. Investment pieces are like the Gold standard. They are always in style. You can wear them for years so spending big money on them pays dividends over time.

5 Ways to Save Money on Investment Pieces

Number One

Go online! Whether you are on the search for the LBD, a trench coat, leather jacket, the Internet is abundant with deals. I'm an avid, supporter of Amazon, GILT, and Zulily.

Number Two

Know what you are looking for. Find it and shop around. Find out who has it and what the lowest price possible is on it. Get the little barcode reader on your phone so you can search it out for the best price.

Number Three

If you know there's a holiday coming up like Easter, Christmas,

Father's Day, Mother's Day, WAIT. Find out if a sale is coming up. Shop on sale often, online and offline!

Number Four

Some retailers only hold online sales. Sign-up for their news-letter so you can stay abreast of when the sale is coming. You may also get a coupon for signing up for their email list. Just remember to unsubscribe when you have achieved your goal to keep your inbox uncluttered.

Number Five

Relationships are an investment that pays off when it comes to shopping. So be nice and make mates with sales associates and managers. I cannot tell you how many discounts I have been given for just being great with people. Associates have alerted me that a sale is starting. I let them know if I am looking for something and usually they tell me when it will be on sale.

STYLISH MUM INVESTMENT PIECES TRACKING LIST

Just like financial professionals track certain stocks, so too the style hunters track the best price for items. Keep this list handy to make sure you don't miss out on a sale. Make note of the best places to shop online, offline, and the right people to know who can give you a heads up.

Item	Store or Website	Contact Name and Details	Price Sales and Dates

9: BE CONFIDENT NOT CONFUSED

Confidence radiates from the inside out. The clothes you wear to match your personal style reflect the inner self assurance possessed by the person. No one can cultivate real confidence in you except you. Coaches, stylists, therapists, and others who are supportive resources can only go so far. I want to stress this fact because you can wear a power outfit worth thousands of dollars but if you're shaking on the inside it will come across. Ever notice how Richard Branson can be commanding while wearing a casual pair of denim jeans and Vest? How does that happen? Confidence.

Style is about bringing out the best version of you. Experts can style a person to the nines but we can't reprogram their mind-set. Confidence is King or Queen. To optimize the effectiveness of your personal style never forget to build your self-confidence daily. I am talking affirmations and beliefs shifting. You have to convince yourself with solid proof that you're worth a million dollars and deserve to look it. Unless you possess authentic confidence you will come across as confused both in body language and style. How to avoid confusion in clothing? Read on.

3 Steps to Guarantee You Always Look Fabulous

Don't rely on me, another stylist, or anyone else to give you the confidence to put clothes together. Once we've gone over the fundamentals of style and gotten rid of all of the stuff you don't wear, you're good to go. If we haven't edited your wardrobe of certain items, we've tailored it so it fits, or we've repurposed it so it's new. We have established a foundational wardrobe. Then pieces that work with your style inspiration was added strategically to enhance your style. Items that we just love or trends we want to incorporate into our day-to-day wardrobe was added.

Cultivating the remainder of your fabulous style on a daily basis is up to you. In the three steps I point out to always look fabulous, the emphasis is on carrying yourself with an abundance of confidence. These are tactics anyone can do.

Let's begin!

Mirror Mirror on the Wall: I'm the Fairest of them All!

Sleeping Beauty's stepmother asked the mirror the wrong question. That fairy tale is an example of how fragile false confidence is. The Queen needed an external object, her magic mirror, to grant her validation. No wonder that the day it replied that Sleeping Beauty was the new "It" girl of the Kingdom, the Queen freaked out. She got consumed with rage and ordered Sleeping Beauty to be done away with. Even when the Queen looked like Charlize Theron in *"Snow White and the Huntsmen"* did she react like a crazy lady who should be in the psych ward. Not a very beautiful sight at all! Don't follow this example.

Step One: Look in the mirror and tell yourself you look good. Come on, now, don't be bashful. Modesty is one thing. Self-reproach is quite another. As busy mums we rarely look in the mirror after we've gotten ourselves together. Once we're dressed it doesn't occur to many mums to take a second and bask in their own beauty. Don't confuse this practice with vanity or narcissism. This is an act of acknowledging self-worth, not becoming a slave to outer beauty.

Step Two: Invest in a floor mirror also known as a full body mirror. Look at yourself. See what you look like. Notice what you look like from all angles. This way, when you leave the house, you know what you look like from all sides. Instead of wondering what people are seeing in the back or what you really look like you will know for sure. Who needs the distraction of being unsure anyway? Not me. Not you. I'm conscious of how I look thanks to my full length mirror. If I run out of the house without looking at myself in the mirror, I spend the day asking myself, "What do I look like? Why is everybody looking at me like that?" All that and wondering over what's going on with your appearance can cause self-doubt to creep into your consciousness. Avoid messing with your own head.

Step Three: Remember that you already know what your style is and it's fabulous on you. There is no room for doubt. You have picked out the ideal clothes for you with that knowledge. You're looking beautiful and you know it. No second guessing! Again, confidence is Queen. Something Sleeping Beauty's mother didn't know and it cost her the throne.

Why Confidence is Queen

Remind yourself until it's established as an unwavering belief in your mind that you know how to put outfits together. No excuses. Be confident. Confidence is the magic elixir that takes you from looking nice to being magnetically attractive. Confidence is 95% of what creates a fabulous personal style. Think of people who can get away wearing things that most others could not. Why? They own it. If you're not confident in what you are wearing, no one else will be either.

Remember too that the most attractive celebrities are often those with genuine confidence. Christina Hendrix and Meryl Streep are perfect role models for the attraction power of confidence. Hendrix is blessed with an abundance of curves in a sea of size zeros in Hollywood. Rather than starve herself to her bones, Hendrix shows them off with style. She often wears form flaunting dresses and accessories that emphasize her curves. The reason Hendrix pulls this off so fantastically is her confidence. She loves her curves and comes across as very appealing for it.

Meryl Streep is in a class of her own in the confidence game. Apart from her numerous Oscars and Academy Award nominations, Streep has been mesmerizing audiences for decades. Since her early 20s, the legendary actress has captivated fans. Ironically, Streep's extraordinary success is a stark contrast to her down-to-Earth lifestyle off-screen. Reality stars with an entourage are reported to display far more Diva behaviour whether on camera or not. Streep distinguishes herself for being so humble because she has genuine confidence. Unlike her contemporaries, Streep still lands major roles, without needing to indulge in numerous plastic surgery procedures to recapture her youthful look. Why? Confidence is timeless and trumps age. Streep is too confident to allow age to undermine her sense of personal value.

One of my favourite actors is Idris Elba. He oozes a strong quiet confidence. Idris can wear a burlap sack and look like the cat's meow. A colleague of mine fancies actor Michael Fassbender who has sometimes been called the male version of Meryl Streep. She finds Fassbender as magnetic off-screen as the X-Men character he portrays, young Magneto.

Fassbender can wear his most casual clothing and still attract people like honey pulls in bees. He too has the best asset in his repertoire: natural confidence. Both Elba and Fassbender come across as being very comfortable in their own skin. That is why the clothes they wear can change but the personal style attraction power remains. Elba doesn't seem to want to be anyone but himself. He is confident in who he is, he doesn't try to imitate Oscar winner Denzel Washington. Same goes for *"Mad Men"* star Christina Hendricks, she doesn't try to diet down to a shapeless size 0. Rather, she loves her curves and shows them off!

Elba's confidence was so apparent that rumours began circulating in late 2014 that he could become the first non-European looking actor to portray James Bond. Fassbender eclipsed Brad Pitt in the film *"Inglorious Basterds"* because he seemed to possess a genuine strong sense of self. Rather than be intimidated by

Pitt's star power, Fassbender held his own, and outshone him. Later on in "*X-Men: Days of Future Past*", he did it again when sharing screen time with Hugh Jackman.

Confidence is knowing who you are and bringing out the best of you for you. Others who appreciate what you present to the world is like icing on the cake. Confusion is the opposite. It's unappealing because a person who doesn't have a clue who they are, seem erratic. Even if they imitate a popular celebrity, their look won't have the same effect. As a result, these people are often not comfortable with themselves, and make others even more uncomfortable. The confidence I described as exhibited by Elba, Fassbender, Hendrix, and Streep are available to everyone. It's going to take work if you struggle with self-acceptance. I can't promise it's going to be easy. Expect to stumble along way. But you must start somewhere.

The Biggest Mistakes Women Make
When It Comes to Style

The biggest mistake a women can make concerning style is thinking they don't need it. Style is like car insurance. When you don't have car insurance that's when you get into an accident. Sure, you could have car insurance your whole life and never get into one. The paradox of life operates like this. If you don't have style that's when you get called for that big interview or huge event. Your immediate reaction is, "Oh my God, what am

I supposed to wear?" Then you spend so much time that morning freaking out over an outfit instead of focusing on the job interview.

Another example is when you are going to have dinner with your spouse or significant other. Despite how romantic the gesture, all you're doing is sitting there wondering, "Oh my God, what am I going to wear?" You're not looking forward to the dinner at all because you are stressing out over what you're going to wear. Personally, every mum should have as many moments as possible having fun, and living life.

Style is just a means to an end: looking fabulous and feeling confident about how you look. Mums have more important things to worry about as it is. You already have enough real stuff to worry about in the morning, during the day, and at night. Real life worries flow. When you are confident and feeling it, things go smoother.

Think about it. You pay your taxes on time so you don't have to worry about it for the whole year. If you have style you don't worry about what you look like. It eliminates distractions like worrying about, "Oh, what am I going to wear to work?" Have confidence in your ability to pick out something that makes you shine. Compare that to some people who lack it. They are the ones who wind up at the Christmas party with the really inappropriate dress that shows as much as it covers. Everyone else just shakes their heads. Meanwhile, you are so thankful it's not you, that person has no style, no idea she looks bad, and no mates, obviously.

Style is who you are. It's an expression of your outer self. The clothes you put on says something about you and who you are to the world. If you're a bum that's what you're going to look like. Confident people have no problem getting themselves together in the morning by doing what needs to be done in selecting attire. I know you want to put your best foot forward. That's why you bought this book. I don't care who you are. I know being your best matters. I also know you don't care what anybody thinks about you, but we agree that you never know whom you're going to meet while out.

I have met all kinds of celebrities, some at the airport, of all places. I mean, really? Why couldn't I have met them at an event or a boutique where I could have struck up a conversation? I meet people everywhere and learnt, even as a military spouse, that when you're that wife or significant other that looks a hot mess all of the time, you don't get invited to a lot of things. If you're that mate that looks like you just rolled out of bed all of the time, your mates won't invite you to go out with them. If you're that sloppy looking employee that never looks together, it could seriously derail your career opportunities. There are top connections at the workplace who may have pegged you as not getting that promotion. Sad, but it's true. That's the society we live in. Humans are very dependent on their eyesight to navigate the world.

More importantly, wouldn't you rather put your best foot forward? Why not be the mum that's together? I know I would. Who wouldn't want to be the mum that other mums wonder, "How does she do it? How does she run a business, take care of two children, and look fabulous all the time?" The answer I give is, "Well, it's because I take care of that the night before and don't have to worry about it in the morning. Style timing means I'm not waiting until the morning to pick out what to wear. I make sure after they go to bed I put my clothes out. I make sure I'm already put together for the next day, so I can devote my full energy to them." Done.

10: SHOW OFF

After reading my book, I'm quite confident that you will know how to dress fabulous with ease every day. You will know how to put yourself together.

What's next?

Now I want you to show off! I want you to look good every day and own it! Like I said earlier, there is nothing wrong with basking in your beauty it is not vanity. What I am talking about is self-love, self-respect, and knowing your value! This is my definition of showing off. Why do you want to do this? How else do you instill self-love in your kids and everyone around you except by example?

So called mates used to say to me all of the time, "Toya, you're just showing off." Showing off is a good thing to me but that wasn't always the case. Showing off had a bad connotation for me growing up. It took me a while to realize that it was natural for me to want to dress up and laugh out loud. So go ahead and show off your fabulous personality to the world.

When someone says you are showing off just wink and reply with, "I know." For me, showing off has a positive intention behind it that benefits others as well. I love me exactly as I am but it didn't happen overnight. Now I want you to love who you are and to show off your inner beauty on the outside.

Doesn't a Mercedes and Porsche commercial show off every time it airs on TV? Don't you feel better at the thought of owning one and doing what it takes to own one? That's what I'm getting at! Beauty has launched a thousand ships, inspired some of the greatest poets and artists to go beyond their limits. Beauty inspires. That is why it is so powerful.

Why I Want Mums to Show Off!

I want you to show off by looking fabulous every day. I want you to embrace the fact that you are beautiful, you're a mum, and someone who does so much for other people. This book is a success for me when you know you're worth it. I want you to know that when you're walking down the street, turning heads is a given, and you make no apologies for it.

Why? You are well put together. You have spent some time on yourself. You are basking in the knowledge of your self-worth and it makes you shine so bright that others are inspired. So show off! Show off without apology or explanation.

The Stylish Mum Manifesto: Closing Comments

I wrote this book because I feel that there's a stigma about being a mum. There seems to be some unwritten rule that mothers can't be stylish, sexy, or exciting. Many women have it in their minds that they can't be that hot mum because there is something wrong with it. Who wrote that rule? Why is it bad? I can't come up with a decent answer, so that's pretty much why I wrote this book. Break the beauty rules that don't empower you!

As a fashion stylist and a mum, so many women come up to me, and said, "Can you help? How do you do this? You look so pretty? Where did you get that?" For something that comes so naturally to me, I quickly realized that it's harder for other people to style as easily. Once I recognised this need, I wanted to put together a really simple, easy guide that offers up all of my experience wrapped in to one book. I wanted it to be a quick and to the point guidebook of everything that I've learned by being a mum and a stylish one.

No matter how busy you are, never forget that you can still look fabulous because you are worth it. Remember, your life is not only about caring for others. You have children and a significant other or spouse that is looking up to you. If you have a daughter, she is definitely looking up to you, and that is where her self-value is coming from.

Besides, don't you want to look good for your spouse or significant other too? If you have a son, he's going to marry someone like you. So raise the bar. I want my audience to know that it's not hard. Style timing makes you look good effortlessly. Now you can be that mum that everybody comes up to and says, "Oh my, you look so pretty today. Where did you get that dress?" or, "How did you put that together?" Plus, you do it with confidence!

All mums deserve to look and feel like a star whether they are a busy working mum, stay-at-home mum, even nannies and grandmothers could probably read this book and get a kick out of it. For anybody who wants to know style and learn a step-by-step, no nonsense guide to looking good, my book is ideal for them.

Thank you for purchasing this book! Please let me know what you think by contacting me via

email: info@toyastyles.com
facebook: facebook.com/ToyaStyles
I would love to hear from you!

Until next time!

Be. Epic.

Toya Styles

ABOUT THE AUTHOR

From Military to High Fashion, Toya Styles is the founder and Chief Fashion Stylist for ChicDivineStyle Consulting, a full styling service & marketing company catering to women with busy, active lifestyles. Her work is well documented in fashion and lifestyle blogs and on PrettyButter.com, and she has been featured in major publications such as the Charleston, ModishMom and Style 31 Magazines as a true trendsetter. Toya is also an Air Force veteran, Air Force wife, and a mother of two. She began styling women in her family since she was little. Now, she provides professional styling for military spouses, models, and CEOs. Her expertise spans the US, European, and Japanese markets. Style is her passion.

CPSIA information can be obtained
at www.ICGtesting.com
Printed in the USA
LVHW112301110419
613928LV00002B/17/P